TIME-TRAVEL GUIDES

The STONE AGE

BEN HUBBARD

Gareth Stevens PUBLISHING

Please visit our website, www.garethstevens.com. For a free color catalog of all our high-quality books, call toll free 1-800-542-2595 or fax 1-877-542-2596.

Cataloging-in-Publication Data

Names: Hubbard, Ben, 1973-, author.
Title: The Stone Age / Ben Hubbard.
Description: Buffalo, NY : Gareth Stevens Publishing, 2026. |
Series: Time-travel guides | Includes glossary and index.
Identifiers: ISBN 9781482475517 (pbk.) | ISBN 9781482475524 (library bound) |
ISBN 9781482475531 (ebook)
Subjects: LCSH: Stone age--Juvenile literature. | Prehistoric peoples--Juvenile literature. |
Civilization, Ancient--Juvenile literature.
Classification: LCC GN768.H78 2026 | DDC 930.1'2--dc23

Published in 2026 by
Gareth Stevens Publishing
2544 Clinton St.
Buffalo, NY 14224

First published in Great Britain in 2022 by Hodder & Stoughton

Artwork and Design: Collaborate Agency
Editor: Sarah Silver

Picture credits:
p.4-5: © johnbraid/Shutterstock.com, p.28: © Vincenzo Iacovoni/Shutterstock.com,

Printed in China
CPSIA compliance information: Batch #QW26GS: For further information contact Gareth Stevens at 1-800-542-2595.

Find us on

CONTENTS

Skara Brae 4
Putting Skara Brae on the Map 6
Meet The People 8
Inside Skara Brae 10
Where to Stay 12
Artistic Interiors 14
Fish and Farm Like a Local 16
Entertainment and Nightlife 18
Stone Age Shopping 20
Skara Styles 22
Tools of the Trade 24
Take a Day Trip 26
Visit Quick! 28
Glossary 30
Further Information 31
Index 32

SKARA BRAE

Welcome to Skara Brae – a Scottish seaside settlement built by Stone Age Britons over 5,000 years ago. Prehistoric people were skilled at making tools out of stone and bone. Here at Skara Brae, people constructed one of northern Europe's first stone villages. Most people living in Britain at this time built wooden homes, but in Orkney there were hardly any trees, so they used stone instead. Now, new time-travel technology has enabled us to journey back to prehistoric Skara Brae and meet these ancient people.

TIME-TRAVEL GUIDES

Your time-travel guide

Congratulations for buying this Time-Travel Guide – the must-have companion for travelers journeying into the past. This guidebook will give you expert advice on where to stay, what to see, and how best to spend your time in the Stone Age. Top travel tips throughout will give you the low-down on what to bring, where to shop and which local delicacies to try.

Today, Skara Brae is a major destination for tourists. The walls of the settlement are still standing, but the roofs have long since gone.

Top Tip

When to go

Travel in summer to avoid the devastating winter storms. These are sometimes so severe they can wash away whole layers of sand and soil from the land.

Guesswork

As the people of Skara Brae left no written words about what they believed or what their lives were like, experts have to make a good guess. They do this by looking at what they left behind, such as their standing stones, tombs, houses, objects, bones, and even their trash. We can only guess at what everyday life was like for the prehistoric people of Skara Brae, especially when it comes to what they believed or felt about things.

Top Tip

What to pack

Insect repellent. In the summer, Skara Brae can be overrun by midges, and fleas have been found there by archaeologists – the first in Europe!

PUTTING SKARA BRAE ON THE MAP

Plan your trip and ensure you never get lost with this map of the Skara Brae settlement and surrounding area. Not sure what to see first? Don't worry – the key areas of interest have been highlighted for you. To find out more about each area, simply turn to the page numbers provided on the map key below.

Skara Brae is considered the finest of the Stone Age settlements found on Orkney. However, it is certainly not alone. People began building stone structures in Orkney from 3500 BCE and its islands are dotted with houses, villages, tombs, and standing stones.

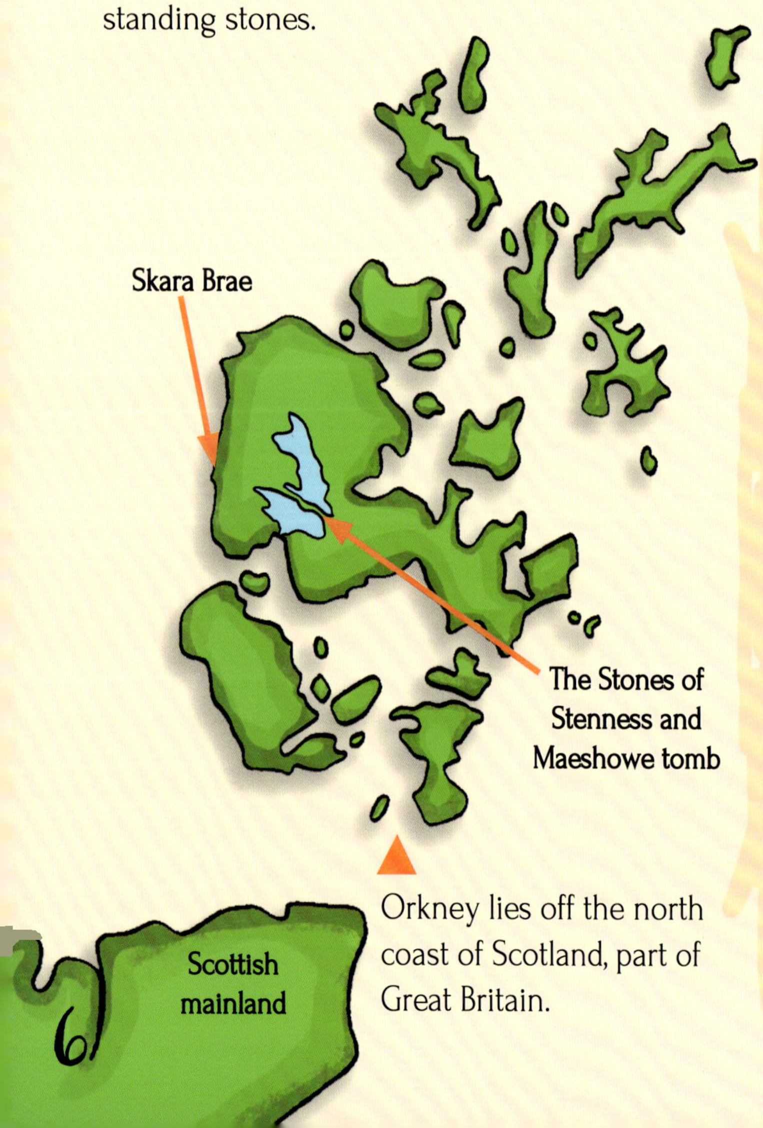

Orkney lies off the north coast of Scotland, part of Great Britain.

The Mainland

Skara Brae is situated on the largest of Orkney's 70 islands known as the "Mainland." The Mainland is also home to the ceremonial Stones of Stenness and a massive tomb called Maeshowe.

Top Tip

What to pack

Comfortable shoes. There are no cars, bikes, or skateboards in the Stone Age, so you'll have to get used to traveling everywhere on foot.

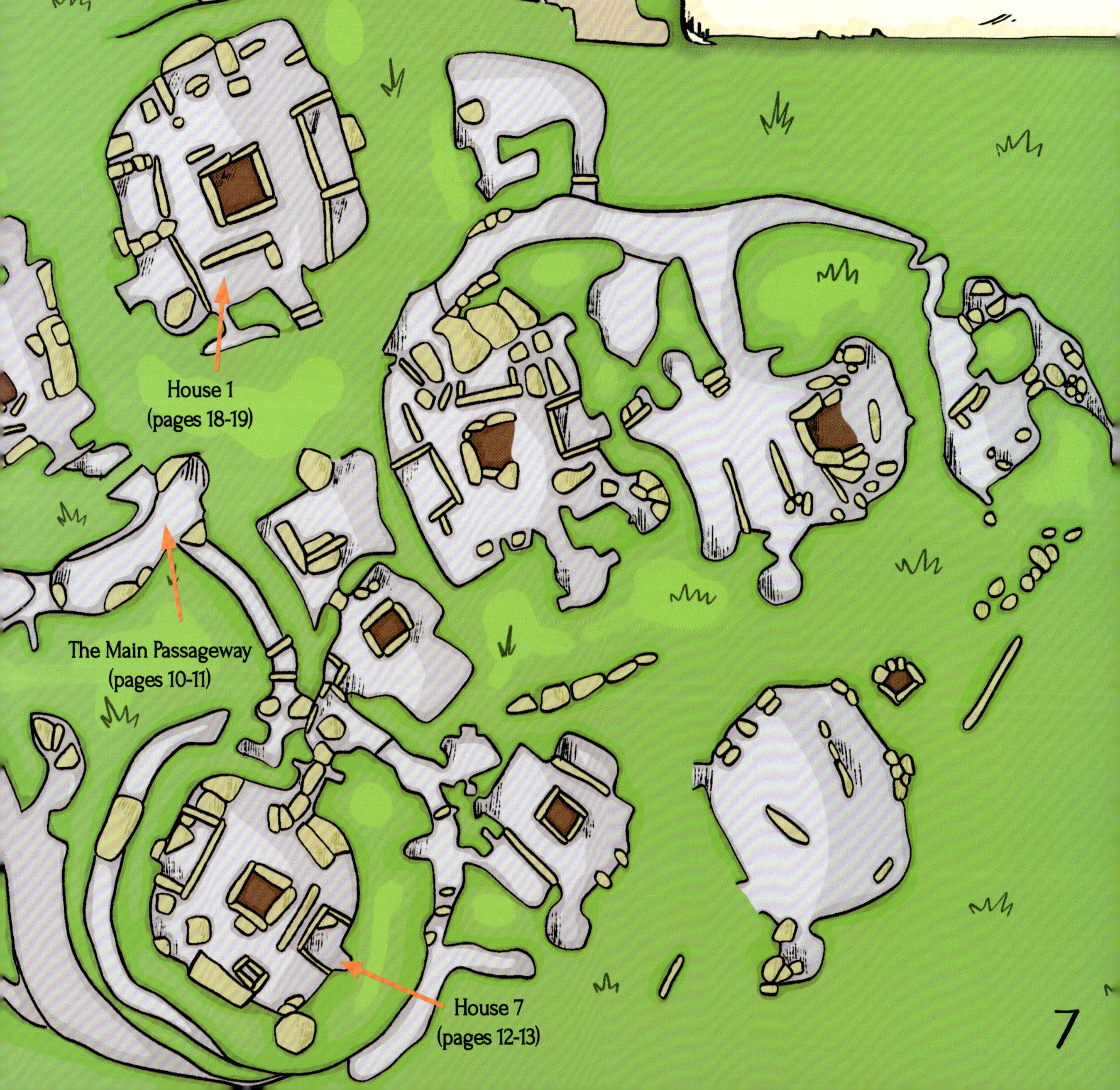

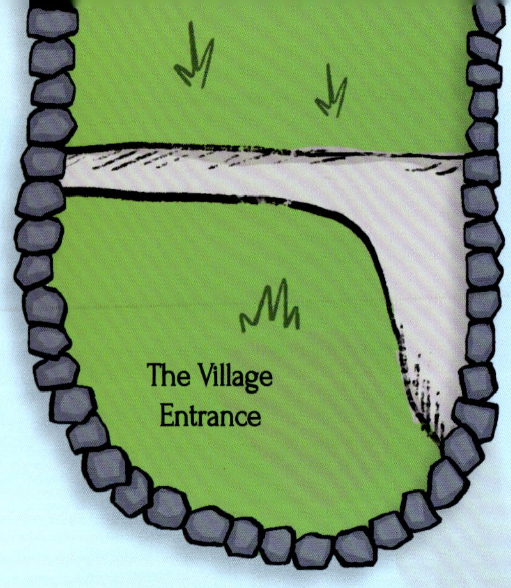

MEET THE PEOPLE

Your journey back in time to Skara Brae starts with a short walk up to the village entrance, where the welcoming residents will be keen to show off their impressive settlement. Built into a grassy hill with commanding views over the sea and surrounding countryside, Skara Brae is the most important feature of the local landscape.

Stone Age settlers

Skara Brae was constructed in around 3100 BCE by settlers from Scotland who were searching for farmland. During this time the world was changing. Instead of hunting and gathering to survive, people began farming animals and growing crops. This is why the period is called the Neolithic, or New Stone Age. After they arrived, the people of Skara Brae set up some of the first farms in Britain. Then, they began to build an entire settlement from stone – Skara Brae. People lived there for around 600 years.

A safe settlement

The residents of Skara Brae are a peaceful people who are on friendly, equal terms with each other and their neighbors. There is no need for weapons here, or even defensive walls. Instead, settlers from all over Orkney meet to trade, conduct ceremonies, or build massive megalithic monuments in their spare time.

Top Tip

Dress for summer

Stone Age Skara Brae is warmer than in modern times. This makes it possible to grow crops such as wheat. It also means summers can be pleasantly mild. Remember to pack your swimsuit and sunscreen.

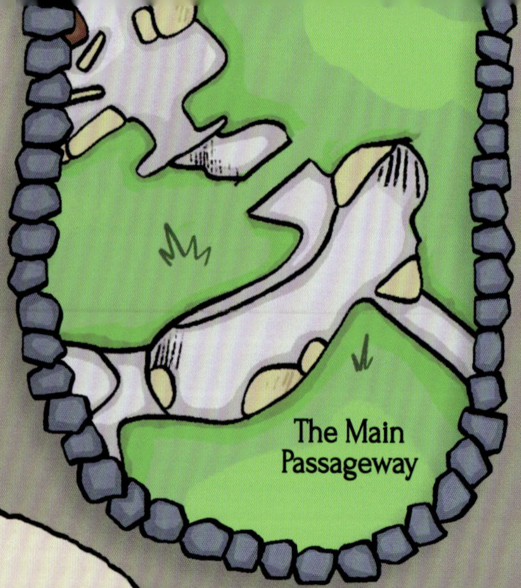

INSIDE SKARA BRAE

From the outside, Skara Brae looks like a hill with stone walls and grassy dome-shaped roofs poking out from the top. This is because the settlement is built mostly underground to block out wind and rain and is covered with grass turf. Once you stoop down to enter the passageway connecting Skara Brae's houses, you will not see daylight again until you come back out.

Top Tip

Watch your head!

Stone Age people are shorter than we are today. As such you will need to watch your head on the low ceilings at Skara Brae. As well as being shorter, Stone Age people do not live very long. The average lifespan is only around 40 years.

Midden made

Skara Brae is built into a hillside made of trash. This trash consists of bone, shell, stone, and animal dung discarded by the first people of Skara Brae. Over many decades, the trash rotted away until it became a material called midden. This midden formed large mounds, which the villagers then carved into to make seven houses and connecting passageways between them.

They strengthened these structures with stone walls and covered them with grass turf roofs. The completed hill-shaped construction ensures the settlement of Skara Brae is solid, strong, and protected from the weather.

A village on a village

The settlement of Skara Brae you are visiting today is actually built on top of an even older village. This is because, over time, the growing population at Skara Brae decided to build larger and more modern homes. At its peak, around 100 people lived at Skara Brae.

WHERE TO STAY

Book early to rent one of seven popular Skara Brae holiday homes available for time-travel tourists. Each home consists of a cozy single room, stylishly decked out with the latest Neolithic furniture and fittings. Here, you can pull shut the solid stone door for privacy before settling down to sleep on a genuine stone bed.

Easy storage

All Skara Brae homes have small storage alcoves, or shelves, built into the wall. However, those travelers willing to spend a little more can have a larger alcove used as an inside toilet. There is no flusher, but water running through a drain underneath does just as well.

Top Tip

Let the fire burn low

The hearth is the central point of every Skara Brae home. It may be tempting to keep a roaring fire going all night, but with only one ceiling ventilation hole this can make your holiday home very smoky. Instead, let the fire burn down before bedtime.

A solid draft-stopping door

A Skara Brae door is a large stone slab, which you'll need to heave into place to block the entrance. A bar made of whalebone or wood then locks the door by fitting into slots on the walls.

Slumber on a stone sleeper

A bed built from stone slabs may look uncomfortable at first sight. However, your Skara Brae bed will be transformed with a traditional mattress of heather and bracken, and animal skins for warmth. Beds come in two sizes – small and very small.

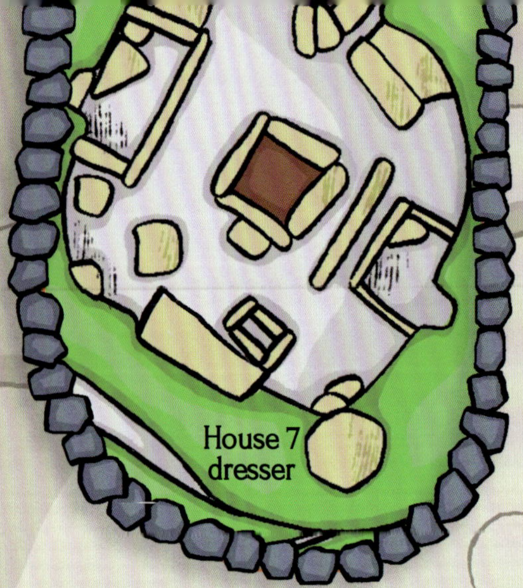

ARTISTIC INTERIORS

The people of Skara Brae are extremely proud and their homes are adorned with the latest objects and artistic decoration. Wall carvings and unusual small stone objects give an engaging glimpse into the creative craft of this Neolithic community.

The dresser display

The most fashionable piece of Skara Brae furniture, the dresser, is in a special place in every home. Kept on display here are the owner's most treasured possessions: small, carved balls and other stone objects with grooves and geometric patterns. Not only pretty to look at, these objects are also used in rituals and ceremonies (see pages 26-27).

Take a closer look: stone ball

A symbol of power and prestige, this stone ball took many hours of skill and patience to complete. There are no metal tools in the Stone Age, so the ball's pyramid-shaped knobs had to be carved using stone hammers, sand, and water. Similar stone balls are made in other Neolithic settlements in Scotland and Ireland.

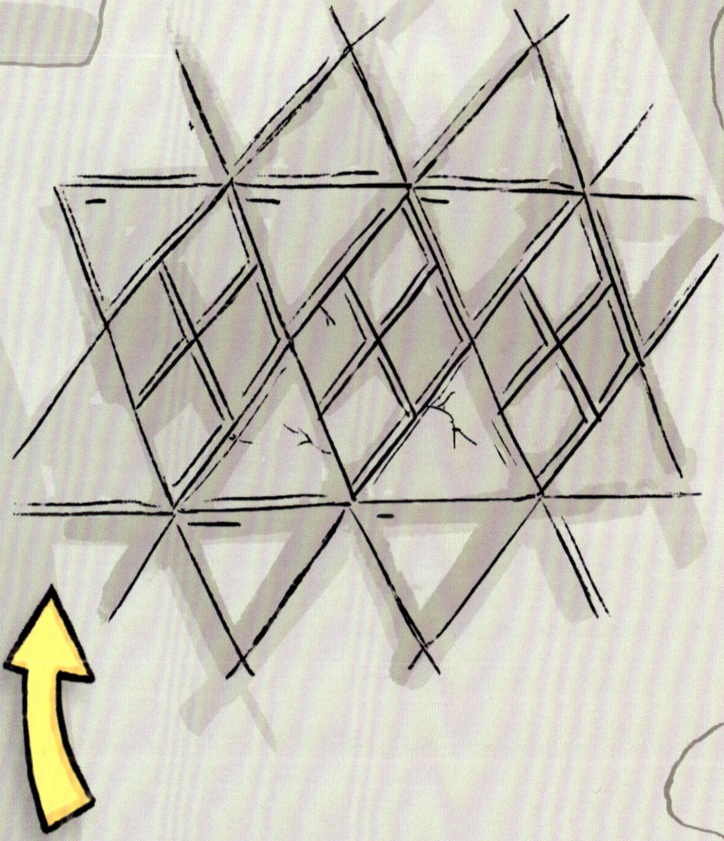

A cover of carvings

Many of the walls in Skara Brae homes have been inscribed with carvings and lined patterns. Some have also been colored with ochre paint. The markings are decorative but also hold many different meanings. Only your hosts can explain what these are, so be sure to ask!

FISH AND FARM LIKE A LOCAL

The people of Skara Brae are farmers and fishermen and everyone in the village helps with the growing and gathering of food. This is the finest, free-range produce around and it comes fresh from the fields into the cooking pots. Why not join in with your hosts and lend a hand bringing in your dinner?

Farming firsts

As the farming pioneers of Britain, the people of Skara Brae are proud to keep their own pigs, sheep, goats, and cows. These animals are used for meat, milk, and material for clothes. You can help herd the cattle or maybe harvest the barley and wheat, which is grown for Stone Age bread and beer. Hauling water from the loch to the village is always appreciated!

A fishy foodstuff

Seafood and fish caught from the ocean and loch make up the common diet. Cod and saithe are the favorite fish, but lobsters, oysters, sea urchins, and crabs are also consumed in large quantities. Whale meat is sometimes eaten, if a creature is found stranded on the shore. The bone and shell left over from the seafood is used for midden and other building material. Why not try eating like a local and tossing your leftovers onto the midden pile?

Top Tip

Missing meat?

For those time-traveling carnivores craving red meat, local hunters can provide deer, boar, and vole on request. A vole is a small mouse-like rodent that might not seem like much of a mouthful. Stone Age roasted voles, however, are delicious!

Top Tip

Cracking egg collection

Seabirds and their eggs are a local Skara Brae delicacy that you might – or might not – be tempted to sample. However, collecting this food can be a perilous task that involves climbing up sheer cliff faces. As there are no modern ropes or safety harnesses in the Stone Age, this is best left to the experts!

ENTERTAINMENT AND NIGHTLIFE

Skara Brae residents are hospitable folk who enjoy sharing an authentic Stone Age evening with modern visitors. Join them for a night around the hearth and enjoy the cozy, dark, and sometimes smoky atmosphere. Partake in popular pastimes such as games and storytelling.

Smoky center

In Skara Brae, the hearth is the center of all household activity and used for cooking, heating, and providing light. Skara Brae houses have no windows and only one small ventilation hole at the top of the roof where fish and meat are often hung to be smoked and cured. You might find the evening a little smoky – and smelly!

Feed the fire

The fire is a welcome comfort from the howling winds outside and your Skara Brae hosts will keep the flames fed with bracken, seaweed, dried animal dung, and driftwood. There aren't many trees in Skara Brae, so wood is a precious material kept to make tools and household objects.

Top Tip

Look out for limpets!

Waterproof stone boxes next to the hearth are used to soak limpets, or sea snails, to soften them for use as fish bait. Be careful not to stick your foot in a limpet box by accident!

Games and gods

Games played with knucklebones and dice are popular pastimes at Skara Brae. Storytelling is another great favorite. There is no written language in Skara Brae, so stories about the people, their ancestors, and their beliefs are passed down through word of mouth.

STONE AGE SHOPPING

Skara Brae is on a well-known Neolithic trade route and people travel from all over to grab the latest bone beads and Grooved Ware pots. Get in quick to bag yourself a bargain – but remember to bring something to barter, or swap, in exchange. Money has not yet been invented in the Stone Age.

Marketplace meeting

The Marketplace is an uncovered area created as a gathering place. Here, village meetings are held, visiting travelers are greeted, and goods are brought in from the nearby workshop to trade. This is a great place to meet people from neighboring Neolithic settlements, and further afield as well.

Take a closer look: Grooved Ware pots

Skara Brae is famous for its flat-bottomed Grooved Ware pots, which are scored with lines and patterns. The pots are often used to drink from, especially during religious rituals and ceremonies. Grooved Ware has become Orkney's must-have tableware over the last few decades. Those still using the older, curve-bottomed Unstan Ware are considered terribly old-fashioned.

Import and exports

While Skara Brae's Grooved Ware pots are popular abroad, its residents are just as keen on the exotic goods brought in by traders from far-flung places. These include volcanic glass jewelry from Scotland's Isle of Arran and ivory pins from Ireland.

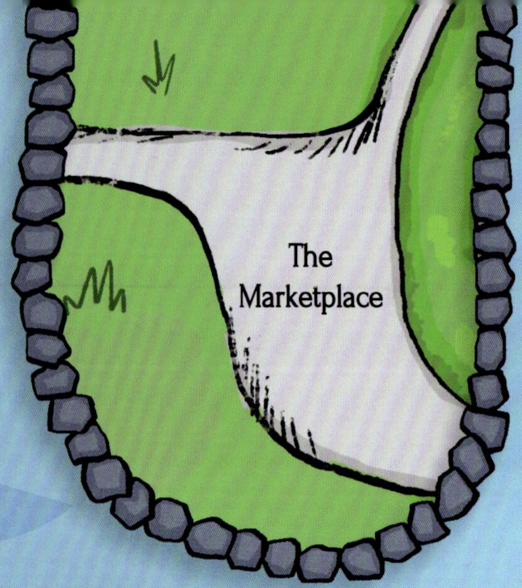

SKARA STYLES

People from Skara Brae are considered market leaders in clothing and jewelry. Their wardrobes have to be functional as well as fashionable. This means using animal skins, as people have done since the Stone Age began. However, the recent addition of ochre and sewn-on jewelry has breathed new life into Skara Brae outfits.

Skins and furs

Because spinning and weaving have yet to be invented, the people of Skara Brae make do with standard Stone Age clothing made from animal skins and fur.

By using bone needles, these materials can be sewn together in a dazzling array of styles. Look out for the latest craze currently hitting the marketplace: otter fur trim attached with walrus ivory needles.

A splash of color

The browns, grays, and beige colors associated with bone and animal skin are sometimes considered drab. To add some eye-catching color, the people of Skara Brae use a splash of red ochre. This is a rust-colored clay pigment mixed with animal fat in a pottery bowl and added to both clothes and bodies for decoration.

Beads and jewels

Skara Brae people are experts at making beads from the teeth and bones of marine mammals. These beads are commonly tied into necklaces and sewn on to clothing in ornamental decoration. Thousands of these beads are made every year, both to trade and also for use at home.

TOOLS OF THE TRADE

Situated next to the marketplace, the workshop is a communal area where Skara Brae craftspeople come to work. Only the latest technologies are used here: stone axes and bone awls. Why not try your hand with these cutting-edge tools to work leather, scrape hair off animal skin, and make needles from walrus tusks?

The workshop

The latest building to be constructed at Skara Brae, the workshop, is the first structure not be carved into a mound of midden. Instead, it stands entirely above ground with extra thick walls to protect it from the weather. There is no furniture in the workshop, but a large hearth keeps it warm inside.

Top Tip

Leave your pocketknife at home

The sudden appearance of steel 2,000 years before iron is discovered may confuse your hosts – or even make them jealous! So, leave your pocketknife at home.

Awls and axes

If you join in at the workshop, your day will involve using a flint axe to carve awls and needles from the bones of farm animals and marine mammals. An awl is a sharp tool used to puncture holes in animal skins. If you don't fancy making bone tools, why not try scraping the hair off animal hides and sewing them together to make clothes?

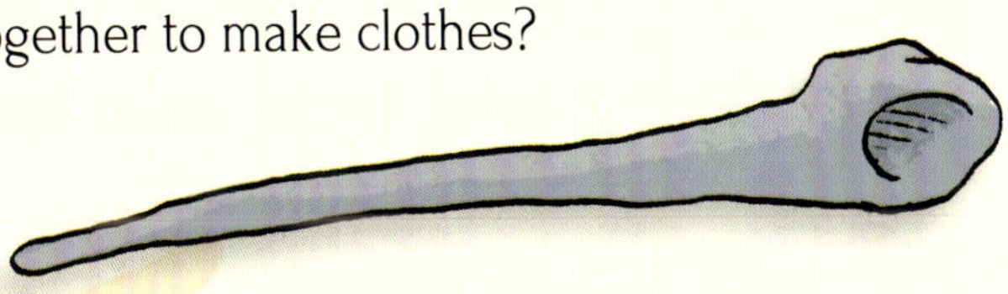

Tools make tools

In the Stone Age, metal is unknown. However, stone axes and knives made from flint have a surprisingly sharp cutting edge. In Skara Brae, these stone tools are used to make smaller tools from bone and wood. Considered the most high-tech tools of Neolithic Britain, these objects are seldom found outside Orkney.

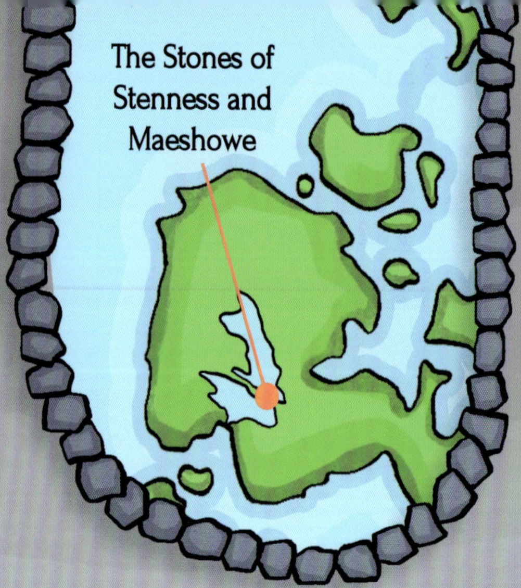

TAKE A DAY TRIP

Skara Brae is not the only must-see spot for time-travel tourists in Orkney. While you're there make sure to visit the other Neolithic sites in the area. These include the massive tomb of Maeshowe and the stunning standing stones at Stenness.

The Stones of Stenness

The Stones of Stenness is a "henge" monument typical of those found in Stone Age Britain. A henge is a circle of tall, thin standing stones surrounded by a ditch. People from all over Orkney worked together over several years to raise the 41-foot- (12.5 m) high Stones of Stenness. The site is used for important rituals and ceremonies and its central hearth may be used to burn animals sacrificed at these events.

Maeshowe tomb

From the Stones of Stenness it is a brisk walk to the tomb at Maeshowe, a mound of soil rising majestically into the air. Only recently built, the tomb has a long passageway that leads to its four chambers. This is where the dead are laid to rest. The tomb has been specially designed so the main chamber catches the last rays of the sun in midwinter.

Rituals and beliefs

The inhabitants of Skara Brae worship many different gods who they believe control aspects of their daily lives. Rituals and ceremonies are performed for these gods, as well as to the sun, the moon, the changing of the seasons, and to honor the dead. The importance of ancestor worship is why such an elaborate tomb was built at Maeshowe.

Top Tip

An eye out for imitators

As the Stones of Stenness was built centuries before Stonehenge, some believe it was the inspiration for Britain's most famous megalithic monument. Keep your eyes open for interested people with strange accents – they could well be the ancestors of the Stonehenge architects!

VISIT QUICK!

Skara Brae has quickly become a popular destination for time-travel tourists. However, the climate is getting colder and villagers are beginning to leave. Therefore, make sure to visit now before the settlement is abandoned and covered with sand.

Changing climate

Skara Brae at its peak was a warm paradise with fertile soil and plenty to eat. But, around 2500 BCE, the climate began to change. It became colder and the sea grew closer, as the waves eroded the nearby cliffs. Salt water invaded the freshwater loch and sand blew into the houses. After a while, the land became less fertile and it became impossible to grow crops such as wheat. This might be why the settlement was abandoned, but nobody knows for sure.

Once you've traveled back in time to Skara Brae you can visit it today to check out the changes.

Changing culture

Skara Brae was a close-knit community for about 600 years, where people were more or less equal. But as the Stone Age wore on, the structure of society changed. Strong tribal leaders emerged who could command groups of warriors. Then, metal weapons and tools were developed as the Stone Age became the Bronze Age. Families could now farm by themselves, without relying on the village for help. Young people from Skara Brae gradually moved away and the village was eventually abandoned around 2500 BCE.

Skara Brae rediscovered

In 1850 a great storm unearthed Skara Brae, which had lain under many feet of sand and earth for several centuries. It was an amazing discovery, which showed that Stone Age Britons lived in civilized communities that were capable of technologies such as inside toilets. This type of plumbing was not seen again in Britain until the time of the Romans, who invaded in 43 CE.

Another storm uncovered more of the settlement in 1925. Work to excavate the site began in 1927 and archaeologists were excited to discover a whole village lay buried beneath their spades.

GLOSSARY

Carnivore An animal that eats meat as opposed to a herbivore, which eats plants.

Ceremony An event that celebrates something, such as an achievement, anniversary, or religious occasion.

Curing A way of preserving meat so it can be kept for a long time without rotting.

Delicacy A type of food that is rare or expensive.

Flint A type of very hard gray stone used in prehistoric times to make tools.

Geometric A pattern made of straight or curved lines, circles or squares, often used in decoration.

Grooved ware A type of pottery made in Britain during the Neolithic period.

Ochre A natural pigment found in the earth and used to dye cloth or paint walls.

Prehistoric Used to describe something that existed at a time in history before information was written down.

Megalithic Very large stones used as monuments by prehistoric cultures.

Monument A structure that is built to remember a person, time or event.

Neolithic Period also known as the New Stone Age that began in Britain around 4000 BCE and ended in around 2200 BCE.

Ritual A series of actions that are always performed in a fixed order, especially as part of a religious ceremony.

Settlement A place where people live together as a community.

Stone Age A period that began around 3.3 million years ago when the first human beings started developing stone tools.

Technology New machinery and equipment developed using scientific knowledge.

Tourist A person who visits a place for pleasure.

Ventilation A way of bringing air into a room or building, such as a hole in the roof.

FURTHER INFORMATION

Books

The Stone Age by Yvette LaPierre (Core Library, 2025)

Stone Age Beasts by Ben Lerwill (Walker Books, 2025)

Websites

Discover more facts and see more photos of how Skara Brae looks today at:
www.natgeokids.com/uk/discover/history/general-history/skara-brae/

Watch videos and do activities to learn about the work of archaeologists at Skara Brae:
www.bbc.co.uk/scotland/learning/primary/skarabrae/

Get information about visiting Skara Brae here:
www.historicenvironment.scot/visit-a-place/places/skara-brae/

INDEX

balls, stone 14–15
beads 20, 23
beds 12–13
beliefs 19, 21, 27
burials 7, 26–27

ceremonies 9, 14, 21, 26–27
climate 9, 28
clothing 16, 22–23, 25
cooking 16, 18–19
craftspeople 14, 20, 24–25
crops 8–9, 16, 28

diet 16–17
doors 12–13
drains 12, 29
dresser 14

entertainment 18–19

farmers/farming 8–9, 16–17, 28
fishermen/fishing 16–17, 19
food 16–19
furniture 12–15, 24

hearth 12, 18–19, 24, 26
houses 5–7, 10–15, 18–19, 28
hunter gatherers 8

Ireland 15, 20–21

jewelry 20–23

lifespan 10
limpets 19

Maeshowe tomb 6–7, 26–27
map 6–7
Marketplace 6, 20–22, 24
mattresses 13
midden 11, 16, 24

needles, bone 22, 24–25

objects, carved 14–15
ochre 15, 22–23

passageway, main 7, 10–11
pots, Grooved Ware 20–21

rediscovery of Skara Brae 29
rituals 14, 21, 26–27

skins, animal 13, 22–25
standing stones 6–7, 26–27
Stonehenge 27
Stones of Stenness 6–7, 26–27
storytelling 18–19

toilets 12, 29
tombs 6–7, 26–27
tools 4, 15, 18, 20, 24–25
trade 9, 20–21, 23

workshop 6, 24–25